BIRTH OF A MURAL

Birth of a Mural

POEMS

Hiba Heba

2023
GOLDEN DRAGONFLY PRESS
AMHERST, MASSACHUSETTS

FIRST PRINT EDITION, January 2023
FIRST EBOOK EDITION, February 2023

Copyright © 2023 by Hiba Aamer
All rights reserved.

Cover portrait bust sculpture of young woman by Billie Bond, inspired by the ancient Japanese art of Kintsugi.

Layout by Alice Maldonado
Set in Gill Sans MT and Garamond Pro

No part of this publication may be reproduced or transmitted in any form or by any means, electronic or otherwise, without prior written permission by the copyright owner.

ISBN: 978-1-7370545-5-9

Library of Congress Control Number: 2023931263

Printed on acid-free paper supplied by a Forest Stewardship Council-certified provider. First published in the United States of America by Golden Dragonfly Press, 2023.

www.hibaheba.com
www.goldendragonflypress.com

For My Mother, Humera;

The Nightingale of Fortitude

*I've got a magic charm
That I keep up my sleeve,
I can walk the ocean floor
And never have to breathe*

— MAYA ANGELOU, *Life Doesn't Frighten Me*

CONTENTS

I

Prelude	3
Waterlogged in Winter	4
House of Dissociation	5
Temporal Glitch	6
Portrait of a Photographer as a Historian	7
The Vicissitudes of Self	8
Life from a Windowsill	9
A Speck of Dust on the Glass Pane	10
Things I am in Love with this Moment	11
Dissecting the End of My Day	13
The Caged Bird Rehearses before it Sings	14
Morning Prayer	15

II

The 'Over-Sensitive' Child Breaks Silence	19
What We Choose to Do on Sleepless Nights	20
Eid ul' Fitr	21
Bread Crumbs	22
Nascence	23
Empty Threat	24
Remember Who You Are	25
Birth of a Mural	26
Homage to our Beloved Abandoners	27

A Postcard from My Mother Who Met Death in the
    Most Startling Way   28
Remanence   29
Desiderium   31
Shrill Light Softens   32
Erasure   33
A Symbiotic Dream   34
Bridge of Fireflies   35
Outro to Grief   36
Penumbra   37
Ghost Town   38
Coronacation   39
Ode to a Nurse   40

III

Crescendo   45
Cloudage   46
Clamped   47
Effacing   48
Dysphoric Heart   49
Patriot   50
Hatching   51
The Dame of Fortitude   52
Domesticated   53
"7-Year-Old Girl Raped in Rawalpindi" – a news headline
    from the year 2020   54
The Geography of our History   56
After Years of Dormancy   59
The Nightingale of Kashmir   60

Body Speaks Two Languages	61
Wedding Mashup	62
Self-Portrait as a Genderless Woman	64
Anthem of the Rebels in the Night	65

IV

Verbis Diablo	69
Blue Moon	70
Kill the Refugee	71
Origins of Humankind	73
The After-World	74
Friday Night on Murree Road	75
Strange Objects in the Sky	76
Renascence of Destruction	78
Remembering a Repressed Memory	79
Mindful Breathing	80
Acknowledgements	81

I

PRELUDE

Let the fire crackle in this glass,
the water rippling,
this cricket-silence you sip.
Your shoulders perish on an old wooden chair;
dusty and historical, impregnated with bygones
who are now a future, nearing.

Entirety was just ten seconds
on this brittle chair, with shoulders
drooping like the insides of a lotus,
head bowed down, hair entangled
in the shoelaces.

A sun grows somewhere, for you.
A gleam enchants your final journey.
This perturbing captivation; your
eyes howl with that last realization:
hope is waiting.
Lift your head up, and plummet
into this welcoming incongruence.

Sometimes straightening a nail in the chair
brings back a progeny of bliss,
returns to you the great beyond,
so you wield the hammer.

WATERLOGGED IN WINTER

My grandmother recites verses from Quran;
decorating her euphonies with praises
for the creator who is pouring buckets
of blessed heavenly water on his worshippers;
a gift of hail-bath to prove his mercy,
but what is merciful about these unrewarded wails?
My aunt says her heart implodes with غم ;
a different flavour of defiance;
a tremor in the clearing of a memory.
Like the casual transience of a lunar halo,
a cruel unfamiliarity comes and goes
in the raucous downpour of winter rain.
My aunt builds a home for her sorrows
in the silky estuaries of the pillowcase, she says;
winter rain is the last cry of a wilted petunia.
But grandmother continues to pray; entranced
by the cataclysmic tendencies of the weather,
her eyeballs swirling like a whirling dervish, she sings:
sodden leaves falling from the trees are ever-moving
wheelbarrows of renewal, even for your voiceless aches.

غم /gham (Urdu): sorrow

HOUSE OF DISSOCIATION

I want to write a story
I could read to the disinterest
that's impaled inside my gut.
The crows look into my pupils,
black-beaked Israfil,
Bleak – a word in my head,
a faint sound in my gasps,
I try to pronounce it
with my idiolect;
a tireless cannibal I tame;
ropes, chains and whips.

Under the lampshade,
a book isn't holy or cursed,
my braided tresses wipe
the crude ink of meaning,
I feel my toes, twitching beneath
my thighs.   It's extraordinary,
to move a part of myself,
to come back to wherever this is
with an easeful involuntary jerk.
Voices in this chest are a shield of
glaucoma for Israfil's soulful trumpet.
I turn the page with
the spit on my index finger,
because now I can.

TEMPORAL GLITCH

Languid air reeks of moss, canopies tinker with clouds,
windless spirits blend then submerge, gravity diminishes;
levitates through a warped sense of freedom; of liberation
chalked on gravels of road, and grass (like solidified brush
strokes) worships slowness: loud slowness, thunderous slowness,
meaningful morphemic slowness. Somewhere beneath thick
follicles thick blood is stridulating, bugs begin to clot in
their tiny abodes.

Time cracked a joke or smoked pot

then stiffened its jaws
to resemble a fossil,

and remained.

PORTRAIT OF A PHOTOGRAPHER AS A HISTORIAN

Travel back to a still shot, it has an earthly existence;
babbling blobs of spellbound hibiscus and thistles.
The photographer is not naïve; she scours every
starlit vision before snapping it between her fingers,
between the whorls of breath. She has always known
nature to be infused with unexplored terrains and levees
and footnotes to past lives. The rustling of every lost
artefact, the cold hush of a Harappan language.
How rusted is history, to be called a rustic beauty?
All that is gone is an improbable threat, like a muted mural.
The photographer is caught between erasure and exposure.
A great old oceanic sound erupts in her uvula:
who is Frankenstein, the panoramic landscape or its
motionless silhouette?

The lifespan of a shot is akin
to a gash that has already bled. Every creation is a musical
dribble on the windshield, wiped away when conceived;
artistically willed into depletion. The key is to take as many
still shots, to taste the rum on the photographer's tongue,
to call god ancient and benign. Answers hanging like weary
autumnal boughs. A man-made object is dead, is redolent
of a cosmic peculiarity. There is nothing to unearth from
wreckage. All history-makers, photographers, artists
and dancers cherish a shared memory: they danced around
campfires to perish in the lucid after-echo of cymbals.

THE VICISSITUDES OF SELF

Coffee is cold, of course.
Bedspread is ceaselessly rebelling against the mattress.
Mirror is scarred with lipstick and foundation,
speckled with loose powder, of course.
Phone is forgetting the loops of this index finger.
Body is unfurling inside a barbed wire.
A punching bag is putrefying beside the book shelf,
'EVERLAST' is etched on its stiff exterior, of course.
Body is made of the dust on a coffin.
Junk food wrappers, cardboard cut-outs, cola cans;
phosphenes in the dark, of course.
Body is a charred mackerel squirming under the saran wrap.
Dreams are dingy. Most of the litter is bred from food, of course.
Click the lighter, light up the moon-kissed candle.
There are ways to reclaim the tactility of a touch.
The same coffee cup, when microwaved,
becomes a Mjolnir in the dome of the palm, of course.
Body is a fortress of mist reviving a dead rivulet.
Body is that gentle glimmer wafting around the burnt
midnight oil, like a believer returning from an umbra.

LIFE FROM A WINDOWSILL

So many names for the unseen:
love, god, future, virus.

The neighbour's window is hosting a carnal banquet.
A woman steers a stroller in the street below.
Her hijab's a cyan gambrel.
Her baby coos at invisible things.

Eyes spaced out.

Zest in the minuscule sockets of its palms.

From a window, there is no vision undetected,
every story is a fleeting image;
a blurry aerial shot.
A man slurps Crème brûlée.

Even the bobbing heads express a history of escape.
So much is left to be defined by the geography around.
The believer and the murderer cross pathways:
two nuclei of a zygote.

60% of water in the bodies floating over the puddles.
The street is a thin philtrum, is an ocean.
Humans are endless pavements;
steering clear of cars and velocity,
made of gills and snorkelling gear.

The nameless is daunting,
but the unseen wields animosity;
lures a ponytailed girl to that dark corner of her room above.

There is no place safer than a fetal position.
Teeth clenched, like the sun in the clouds.

A man slurps Crème brûlée.

A SPECK OF DUST ON THE GLASS PANE

I am lodged in the soil.
So much of what I am is in a fist, clamped
together like a claustrophobic rugby scrum.
I live vicariously through a speck of dust
on my window, a speck that exists without
its own knowledge. My hindsight is an
untamed gladiator in action; every grunt is
a premonition staring at my fickleness through
a frescoed mirror: sometimes a bloodied lioness,
sometimes smaller than the dust speck that has now
left my window. It embarks on a pilgrimage
with djinns and astral travellers: the only creatures
who do not measure time by its density or will,
but by its absence; stronger than the pungent
odour diffused inside a lost haunted manor.
I have a penchant for burying time-travellers
in my vacant eyes. The unsung obliteration within
me stops for a moment to grow trains of cerise
mandevillas around the rugged walls of this manor.
And as I am brought back to the cross-stitches
of regularity, an ice cream cart buzzes in the street,
a tube well is surrounded by men with empty
bottles, sunbeams are shrunken wicks on my eyelashes,
I taste a journey on my tongue. An unread scroll,
I return to the soil louder than riptide.

THINGS I AM IN LOVE WITH THIS MOMENT

Imagination,
a drill in the wall; musical and rambunctious,
like dewy gardenias in his eyes, waning then blooming.
I am in love with the treacherous idea of freeness;
my hair flapping like a country's forsaken flag
outside a car's broken window.
So what if I live inside a bottle?
The bottle is not my home; it's all water and plastic.
I imagine all that is made of water and plastic.
I am in Scotland; the wind is a chorus, beauty
tells self-effacing lies when pronounced beautiful.
All I know is lagoons were never beautiful,
their image is. Stillness is in this multidimensionality.
I am in love with Taylor Swift's All Too Well.
Yesterday I fell in love with Parmesan chicken;
something I never ordered but the waiter forgot
and then it was all I wanted, was he god?
I came home and fell in love
with the fleetingness of Taylor's affair,
her song has 'never return to old blows' inscribed
in its multilingual aches.
My brother gifted me a sunset lamp,
in hopes the changing hues offer a poetic ambience.
He said, "This is for the أمل "
Now this poem's inception has become endless.
I am in love with how my heart bursts into tears
when Daisy hears her name in my voice, drowning
in those cul-de-sacs around the streetlights.
The love I feel is a feeling of recalcitrance.
I am in love with my panic-stricken singing;
an alias that appears out of the eucatastrophes
I forge in my gut, wearing buttoned-up

plaid shirt, wrapped up in an ajrak.
All that looks sacred isn't always sacred.
I am in love with my seven-year-old self who wept
on the chip-flaked staircase, begging to be noticed,
begging to be carried downstairs in firm arms;
a pharaoh's body pulled from the ruffles of a seabed.

آمد /aamad (Urdu): the advent/revelation of a poem
Ajrak: A unique Sindhi shawl

DISSECTING THE END OF MY DAY

Spatula clutched in my hand
and under the sizzling pancakes.
I think of the end of the day;
the last minute before nightfall.
The cakes are henna-coloured now.
There are some distant onomatopoeic
sounds in the twigs of sanober trees.
Maybe the last minute of the day resembles
the liminal space under a bivouac,
stranded at the foothills of the Margallas.
I am there. My eyes envision flying bullets.
Of course, this land is not a warzone,
but it has known war like a blood relative;
our forefathers' displaced smoke signals.
At the end of the day I know how
the day ends, and it isn't a big deal.
Neighbour's barbecue soiree is a movie
I close my eyes to, almost steadily.
The ashen briquettes clonk together,
birthing a noise I can almost see;
a white thread in the night, trapped
in the tarnished contours of the railing.
The sky is a discarded frying pan.

THE CAGED BIRD REHEARSES BEFORE IT SINGS

Papa's antique Sony radio preaches the vacancy around it;
harsh sound of a religious scholar
dampening the mellow call for Fajr prayers.
There are so many ways to declare the break of dawn.
Morning breaths create nebulae over our heads,
weightless water from sprinklers haunts the fern of its longevity.
There is always the phlegm-filled clearing of throat
around shuttered tuck shops; an aubade for the sparrows
who have forsaken their shepherd-like voice
because the ritual of morning songs has long been
replaced with Israfil's trumpet rehearsals.
The stomach churns like the shriek of a kettle;
an alarm to remind our bodies
they are only ours until hunger strikes.
This frequent need to be fed is an heirloom from the maker;
the one who lost himself in the music of his creation.
Papa takes control over the faucet in his hands,
the water drizzles until it's warm, until the skin can bear the heat;
as if this too is a test for endurance.
Bags zip and cars fail to orgasm in their masters' grasp.
We have created so many objects to validate our sentiments.
The cold summer breeze creating welts in our chests,
that one leg hugging the pillow, struggling to let go.
One of us has to run to the kitchen to prevent the chai from
spilling over the stove. Each morning is a cold stab
of mint on our sore gums. That's how the world is restored:
with a cold stab where it hurts the longest.

MORNING PRAYER

I am a whiff of air lingering
      through empty morning streets.
To every corner of a rusty cart,
      to every chair sitting desolate in
the puddle of electric wires:
      I bequeath a future trajectory
of how my life is going to be
      once I am reincarnated as the wind.
The silage of tandoor, fruit shop,
      fruit flies, the masjid tessellations
will remember me as a vagrant
      collecting souls out of tedium.
I have embarked upon the dull task
      of forgetting. I am glad I was born
here, in this meagre town where dark
      cables shroud the beauty of pine canopies
and beetles invade dead dogs on skewed
      pavements. I am grateful that I will tuck
this morning away. How much more is
      there to forget? Each unnamed body ache
is a longing, a jam jar expiring silently.

II

THE 'OVER-SENSITIVE' CHILD BREAKS SILENCE

In first grade when my friend ripped off
a saniplast from his pinkie, I picked up
the forsaken bandage and chose to bury
it in the sand puddles of my schoolyard,
and I went home imagining where the
bandage will go from there; from a junction
between every hushed inhale. Every day
the bandage came back crumpling in my fist;
its sticky interior no more sticky. Every
day I struggled to tie my shoelaces; these
gossamer centipedes, I cried for my fingers'
inability to perform a simple task because
my classmates, the little warlocks, only tapped
that fishtail crust of their laces to perform
the spell. Every carapace of daily chores; an
almond exploding between their molars, water
trickling their throats like a windless swarm
of butterflies, and I would shred and collect my
skins from the domes of dysmorphia, every saniplast,
every snaking lace clotting in my disposition.
The art of butterflying was violently exhausting.

WHAT WE CHOOSE TO DO ON SLEEPLESS NIGHTS

Here I am dipping my fingers
in the misty Lazarus pits of the keypad,
the black mirror fractured in front of me.
A dog squeals somewhere in the narrow street.
My first instinct: save the poor child before it dies.
My lounge and the street below are just two doors apart,
and a bulb-lit staircase; a gambit afloat.
I imagine running barefoot.
Oh but I can't be out this late at night.
Nobody will see me as a lifeguard outside these walls.
If something happens to me it will be my fault;
I chose the audacity of a guillotine over a meadow.
Oh but where is my bra now and the chador.
What would papa think? What would he say?
I sit here, staring blankly at the narcotic black mirror,
asking the quandary that is beheading the horror
of consequence inside me: which life should I save?
The dog answers my question. I am shorn into ease.

EID UL' FITR

Walls were dog-eared, paint peeling off,
the cement was damp as endless rain. Still, outside,
the grape vine draped itself on the railing,
the way mother draped a floral cloth on
the dining table every Eid ul' Fitr. Silk
and satin ribbons of sunset tints, she tied them
wherever old could pretend to be new just
for a day. Every Eid we summoned the skeletons
from our closets, held their brittle bones,
dusted every joint, every ribcage – a hollow
aviary. Chaand raat, and we dunked ourselves
in the tessellations of henna, dreaming who will
have the brightest shade on their palms next
morning; who could win the richest husband in
the future. Jasmine bracelets and fountains of fresh
ubtan erupting in our chin dimples, every vacant
corroding corner of home was coaxed into a fresh start.
Eid told us to be happy, so we were happy every Eid.
Mother's Sheer Khurma untied the knots in our tongues.

Chaand raat (Urdu): The eve of Eid
Ubtan: Traditional beauty mask
Sheer Khurma: Traditional dessert

BREAD CRUMBS

Bread expired yesterday,
so papa gave it to the kuray-wali aunty.
He cannot feed expired food to his kids,
and the garbage collector, wiping sweat
with her dupatta, looked at the bread
as an early morning victory, smiled;
gratitude in the cavities of her teeth.
Kindness can be sneakily serendipitous,
like the sea. Papa opened the fridge,
lentils and boiled rice glared at his
pure heart; three days old, he cannot feed
old food to his kids, so he microwaves it
for his breakfast. Our religion taught us to
give and give more, so we give away death
in glossy Tupperware, and we often eat
death to save our kids, and we often have
our breakfast early, thinking bread crumbs
may leave no trail, but our kids hoot and spit
in narrow streets, daring to stand in front
of flashing headlights. Sometimes, papa
effortlessly changes death's trajectory, sitting
in his saggy chair, watching TV, arbitrarily
tracing the shape of remote's buttons, sneezing.
It's true; self-love is often transmogrified into desire,
into a father who keeps saving you like a mother.

Kuray-wali (Urdu): The one collecting garbage

NASCENCE

FOR BILAL AND ABDULLAH

She rolled up the sleeves of her oil-smeared kameez,
let globular chapatti somersault on the dusky skillet;

Mother taught us the meaning of "it's raining cats and
dogs," long before it indigenized itself on our bilingual,

bipolar tongues. We have since, in our seven-year-old
mysticisms, called upon the sagacity of fuchsia-blue

skies. Scampering across half-built brick houses,
summer sweats interspersing with freshly cubed

mango aromas: we dreamed together of torrential
downpour; rain gasping frantically for our steadfast

cloud-nines. Just like that we had wished to possess
all that was undefined from the remaining gossamer

childhood days. Once, in a fleeting moment on
the cemented roof-top, when my brother mimicked

Shoaib Akhtar's signature bowling style: I saw an oblong
rapturous cage soar towards the depths of stratosphere,

and then it rained cats and dogs. We spread our
olive arms; skinny as the sugarcanes of Faisalabad, and

with painless ease we unfurled in the supple creases of home,
like layers of grief peeling away from a stoic man's face.

My brothers whistled their synchronized cue to prepare
for the imminent Wild Hunt, but my cumbersome curiosity

leaned on the corroded railing, wondering what caused
a bulbul bird to shun the freedom of an unhinged flying-cage.

EMPTY THREAT

My brother is trying to reach
into a drawer. It's Monsoon.
The furniture is an adhesive now
like moist mesoglea; a thin film of
hymen for things that don't breathe.
Mother's cooking-voice scours
the sweat-sequined air. We rush
through lunch then supper,
horsewhips thrashing our tongues.
My brother struggles to open
the drawer with a wooden ladle,
mother shouts and absconds into
her chores. "Where is he now?"
"Still grieving his taste buds."
He has a penchant for chewing
bank-fresh notes; tens and hundreds.
Papa's car honk is a whiplash to
adjourn the remaining day's journey.
My brother swallows his crinkled
spit. Mother reappears, zaps past us
in her ironed kurta. The skillet is
aromatized by chapatti, the door mat
surrenders itself to an empty threat.

REMEMBER WHO YOU ARE

It's that time of the year again,
when I seek refuge from the day
by traipsing into the world of Lion King.
My life is a mirror-view then, a sun-fused
face of Mufasa recounting my
shortcomings to me. I trace the wind-free
sapphire sky, search for my own scattered
fragments. I too bear the circle of life
within me, and it often wreaks havoc.
Every constellation has its own
story. Every new moon is unchanging,
effacing into its lunar history.
To me, Lion King is the childish reassurance
every breath needs to live and live on
in its river-gazing algorithms.
My mother said she swam in the Indian Ocean
back when she could swim and sing
in Swahili, that Simba is a lion, my brother
is Simba but I should walk like Sarabi:
too brave for the world yet too afraid. Remember
to only cry in your nightmares. In life be your
own concealer and retinoid. A jarring roar
brings back the children we left behind as souvenirs.
Young Hamlet's homecoming; one can only
hope to feign nostalgia as a method of madness.

BIRTH OF A MURAL

Repetition: a mother rocks her baby in a carry cot.
Her breath fixated on a markhor's head on the wall;
her breath reinventing the dim life of monotony.
There are some unexplored adages in the floral
notebooks of her mind: resistance is to end repetition.
Motherhood rises like dust and falls like an untold history.
Midday: it pirouettes around the question of what to cook;
is there any organ left in the fridge to be boiled for dinner?
To the onlookers, she is a shoal of goldfish and the ripple.
There is a steep gorge nearby; a stream revels in its tirelessness,
the rocks beneath bathing with ultramarine-blue spirits.
The mother picks up a book and teaches her baby the colours
of a rainbow: *VIB…GYOR*. Her child is now old enough
to fill each new void with his mother's face.
This thing has a voice. This thing is where my food is stored;
my mann-o-salwa. This thing loves me with a specific sound,
so I am just a mirror away from discovering the spectre in her eyes.
Her touch the quietness of flora, this thing often burns
the witch lodging inside her; that inward scream like the shadow
of Medusa. There are moments in a day she calls it quits
and dallies to the stream; decanting the onyx-ashes of the witch,
milking that wild sibilant urge to be someone else entirely.
When she breathes through her lungs, she is breathing through
another body, she is fragmenting into a mural, into herself.

HOMAGE TO OUR BELOVED ABANDONERS

Another cedar brown sparrow embodies the
numbness of cinders blinking in a pyre.
Her June hatchlings' chirrups crumble in her
hostile warmth. Bluest wind creatures.
Like a fraudulent beggar suddenly appearing
at your threshold, a premonition always arrives when
lazy summer evenings erase all memories
of pre-existence in homebound birds. Little insect
eaters cradle back and forth in the soft-echoing
departures of their daring dervish mother,
who chooses to flit away; possessing the spirit
of a migrant. Her wild freshness. Her wayward heart.
One should learn to spare this wax-nipping
sparrow and her chiming eccentricities.

Nearby, as a cyclone surges through denial's
bones and arteries, a clueless child wipes dust from
the windscreen, sniffs the earth beneath his
fingernails. What could haunt him for growing up
without endless love? Our beloved abandoners
are born inside glistening ruins of sarcophagi,
worshipped forever by the memories of
countless premonitions. Each ground-kissing
sujud denotes the vastness of a wormhole.

A POSTCARD FROM MY MOTHER WHO MET DEATH IN THE MOST STARTLING WAY

Even the stars are a listless array of suburbs.
Supernova whirlpools and life in light years.
Here, humans are called particles. The smaller the better.
If I write "I miss you," it will denote something rueful in
the language spoken on Earth. Here, it just means I am
giving birth to a lonesome deity between us. I canoe around
Ursa Minor and think of those minor frictions I had with your
papa. It reminds me how we are lost in the smallest of spaces,
how there is only just one big language after all. Here, the sky
is indigo, just the way I wanted; just the way I painted your
bedroom walls a burning sapphire indigo. I am out in the open,
and now there is nothing magical about this sheath of starlight.
And if I were to dig my human nails in the reams of this nameless
realm, I will rob myself of the remaining magic. Here, when I say
"I", I refer to my ten-year-old self in Mombasa; brown like henna,
hair in silk braids, legs continents apart and that green mamba
hissing between my heels, then slithering away. I am now a particle,
so I can be a river or a songbird or a soft hiss. Here, rain brings
no poetic sadness. A tree star lands on my toes. I am not startled.

REMANENCE

Imagine you wake up to a lantern
scorching your cheekbones,
your bed is a gazebo or a pulpit where
sleep does not stop you from ageing,
and there is a gale whistling through
your armpits, you taste the time sashaying
on your tongue. You fear that even if you
close your eyes again the lantern will
scavenge your skin. These unattended
fears cannot just sink into the turmeric-soft
sheets that have lately seized you,
like the day outside. So quickly you count
the names of Bacchus through your hash-breath.
Guilt is another Lofi soundtrack murmuring
in the deep basins of your orgasm.
You think of those confessions, how each lover
blew a wish on your fears to perhaps one day
gape at the auroras in Norway. You know
they are leaving when you hear the omens
concealed in the zips of their pants; that rancid
vacancy they leave behind like traces of semen.
Every day you turn on the bathroom lights, splash
water on the wrinkles loosening your grip on reality.
Today, you choose to fight back with retinol
and cotton swabs. When you remember your
mother, it isn't always her signature biryani recipe
or her words of wisdom cross-stitched
on your tattered shalwars, most of the time
it's the tactics she has left behind like forbidden
trysts: place two cloves in the sugar jar to keep
the red ants away, put clumps of eggshells
in your kitchen to ward off the lizards,

sheets can be a home where you discover
your arms were created to hold each other; left
one fondling the right. Sometimes following
the trail of phosphenes in the lukewarm darkness
of your eyes is enough to shroud all your fears.
If lately you can't swim, don't. You won't drown.

DESIDERIUM

There are different places inside a home we call home.
In this silent blubber of nightfall, I plunge into a futurity,
my fingers stroking the warm wombs of orange rinds.
Streetlights are rippling over the rims of kitchenware,
and I picture our son walking barefoot on pixelated countertops.
Imagination is a whorl of breath. There is vigour in each longing.
A million years from now I will be cooking in the kitchen,
birthing an aroma that allows me to travel back to this
sombre moment of idleness. Our son's neatly brushed scalp
toddling against the rhythm of convulsing streetlights,
his sparrow-soft eyes hungry for biryani or halwa puri.
Food is also transcendental. It fills the crevasses of memories;
a tea cosy on every unwashed gash. I imagine a moment
when I am kissing our son goodbye for school.
His fading footsteps, a stampede on my ribcage.   You.
You are a moon-blanched figment; a sheen on porcelain, against
darkness. Yet to lose you is to emancipate a merry child
into the verbosity of a damaged world. Maybe growing old
is growing comfortable in the gentle beauty of heartbreaks.
Denial is the weight of my fingers thrashing against the dough.
Grief is a soundless droplet of sweat trickling behind my ear;
it is the same river that changes, then travels to future, to a home
that fails to surrender the comforting progenies of suffering.

SHRILL LIGHT SOFTENS

This poem started with flood,
not the image, just the word seeping through every object.
The song playing in the background
by The Midnight is a constant splintering in my ears;
the loss that comes with hearing.
Flood: the packet of rusks on my desk,
too many pens like pointed crowns in a holder,
a calendar reeking of stillness, of staleness.
There is just one delicate cup sitting upright in its saucer
like a corset over a wedding dress,
I ask myself, why does it look so civilized, so British?
The teacup, why does it scream attunement?
Two things are always meant for delicate things,
one: they are placed so high on the shelf, like a climber
revering her view from the Babusar top,
two: any delicate thing that reeks of too much faithfulness
is gently pulverized, gently, gently, gently...
look how my neck is swaying,
so gently, I am being pulled away from the flood
and the feminine panache of the teacup,
am I drifting to a place where the shrill light softens?
What do I call this place? The liminal stage,
a ruptured verse, a dam that is dry but wetter than my eyes?

ERASURE

When my cat died,
I didn't sleep at night,
at two in the morning
I brewed coffee.
I prepared for a harvest,
I let in the sun-crinkled
breeze,
my heart joyfully mourned
a dozen spring songs.
Death is also a ritual
of liberation;
you open the gates
to your house
because now no one
lasts long enough
to depart.

A SYMBIOTIC DREAM

Death is fear, fear ricocheting off the plums and cherries,
fear that cloaks the innocent wish to be the first one
to know you are dead, after dying. A sunlit orchard
signifies spring but is deceptive too, like a lost child.

My baby brother Ibrahim is a necromancer in this
dream, his cries compel nature to deflect its boundlessness.
All the life of an orchard; pecans, almonds, oranges,
raspberries, all the weight of abundance slowly festers,
slowly offers the final prayer to the sun, to the crescent.

In this dream, death is a caricature springing back to life,
it traverses the overripe orchard, mazes become maple trees;
there is no way out, light swells like sweltering craters.
I view this war of life as a dreary sequence to a revelation;
an inviting thump of a decade-old toaster, music of the aftermath.

BRIDGE OF FIREFLIES

Depression always occurs in undesirable ways.
This faucet is as cold as a freshly-dug grave,
you have to will your canary hums into existence.
Unless your body is warm from the salt-water,
you are a hung-over orange bereft of citrus.
Sleep is a foghorn, breath becomes invasive.

You search for joy the way you search for happiness:
a sikka under your pillow, the lullaby-singing fairy
peering at you through the craters of moon, your friend
finally finding that punctured kite around a lamp-post.

You take a trip down the winter-still cemetery to greet
your grandfather for the first time, terror preys on you
until the heroic alter-ego decides this is an adventure.
You tell yourself: it can either reek of death or rose water.
So you grace your grandfather's grave with attar of roses;
building a bridge of fireflies between life and after-light.

You choose to unfurl with a nap in this blanket
of confluence. Any place in the world is your bed.

Sikka (Urdu): coin

OUTRO TO GRIEF

Boredom is a legacy. You crave cigarettes,
if not cigarettes, then a Siamese kitten;
Blueberry, his malleable purrs, if not a kitten
then your own life hung in the billows of lampshades,
this jarring sorrow coiling around you,
like Madhubala's regal twirls in those thousand
ceiling mirrors, the melody of moonlight.
How boringly slow a funeral procession is,
intensive too like the seven minutes Nana Abu lived
before dropping his arm on the spring mattress;
a whispering thud evacuating the last drop
of exultation. A myna with her Tuscan-sun beak
leaves the clay pot aquiver on the windowsill.
There comes a time in the longest day, you get
bored of mourning so you liberate yourself in
a small room, puff a Parliament, think of ways you
could destroy the last Horcrux – that has kept
the day alive – to hungrily let go of this humdrum.

PENUMBRA

We always thought apocalypse
would begin when Gog Magog
exclaim Insha'Allah! But it came to
us in the shape of a trifling crown,
now the skies are a clear periwinkle,
a toddler caws in the dingy alleys, there
is no bloodbath, the shrubbery is not
dredged in shrapnel and there are no
potholes bestrewn with dismembered
corpses, every car that whirs past
the Sunday bazaar has its own story
of death, a man abluted in attar of roses
offers his wife a silk dupatta; touching
her pale rubescent heart like a mask
catching a scintilla of breath from our
mouths, a grandfather carefully trudges
over a speed breaker believing it is a
grave for all the graves left undug, his
white turban a supernal halo, a talisman
girdles around his neck; mourning all
the souls it was supposed to protect
when magic existed to harm even those
who are long dead and erased, he moves
past the street kids playing with water-
filled condoms, he reincarnates a grin.

Dupatta (Urdu): A traditional cloth worn by women to cover their head and chest

GHOST TOWN

Inhabitants are television extras,
their mouths sour with lupine,
earthworms inch through curdled
vistas; en route to a place where
boughs quaver in water, the aqua-blue
shutters of vacant shops, museums
springing from hardened mush,
where do all the sunsets go when
expunged from the larynx?
A hologram with nails protruding
like the omniscient gaze of a gargoyle,
counts the beads on an abacus,
just like that, bodies are annulled;
one after another, it takes a trip
around a ghost town to stand still beside
a virus threat; hands interlocked we lean on
a railing, a bicycle endlessly spirals
on its track like a distraught hornbill.

CORONACATION

A year
A present
A pandemic
A mole on my brown skin
I noticed for the first time,
It wasn't there and then it was,
Minuscule and fragile
Inflating between my knuckles
Like lulled reality.
Lockdown. Curfew. Quarantine.
Netflix avarice, hand-wash.
Humans hurtling inside thick walls
Humans need to be out of the picture
To give humanity some time.

ODE TO A NURSE

The pretty nurse taps her feet,
nibbles the fuchsia colour off her nails,
rests all day in the plastic chair,
cares for her patients' bodies till they bloom
into sedimentary macrocosms.
She interlocks her death-licking fingers,
remembering the fragrance of Shea butter
she stole from a surgeon friend's purse.
Her phone tings,
she whispers texts to her lover,
except the texts do not confess love
in the Bollywood style,
she reminds the time around her
of the rhythm of unreleased pleasure
squirting in her nerves.

Between these lonesome intervals,
Karachi whizzes through her reveries,
sometimes a train foregoes a lunar death,
onion peels chant a mystic spell
in the far offing of ill-grown greenery,
husbands quarrel in tall buildings.
Her hindsight can never forget
these distinct sounds of husbands.

She stares into the effervescent gloaming
of her patients' eyes, knows
which one needs to recite the kalima.
Her mouth chews on cashews
and peanuts, like it's cud.

How cunningly has she earned
the title of a prophet,
sensing the advent of Qiyamah
when a patient gives up his snores.
She knows that lungs hold more
than a thread of breath,
and death too
demands careful nursing.

Kalima (Arabic): formal declaration of faith in Islam
Qiyamah (Arabic): The Day of Resurrection

III

CRESCENDO

Bubble gum girl
hauntingly
serene in a room,
her cotton candy buns
aromatized by the
lulling gaze of a
crescent,
it follows her trail
of book adventures
and mispronounced
words for self,
some pictures are
timeless like rituals:
a vortex of neon clouds,
quietude,
a gaping crescent
and the paleness
of her lover's sweater,
she escapes the tremors
of her lover's falsetto
every new moon,
"read me," she implores
the palmists staring at
her from the vintage
dog-eared pages,
the lone moonwalker,
she dreams of grass
on moon; fluorescent
thin threads like
filigree

CLOUDAGE

I see you.
Like me, you're
misshapen;
a swamp in a dwelling.
We merge; a suture
quivers through us,
the way nightmares
take long strides on
still waters.
We're camping
under the mellow lilt
of our alibi; the breath
checks out.

CLAMPED

Now steamy clouds secrete fluids of tranquil appeal, outside.
Nature's another hysterical outburst. Heart pounds.
Damp, humid aerosols. Monsoon comes home.
A well-rehearsed play; thunder grunts,
spider veins protrude from the valleys of sky.
Sounds of water tiptoe in potholes,
spanking and pinching the sidewalks;
softened mush.

The air conditioner is set to 17°C.
Light chiffon shawl massaging these shoulders
and green-tea to enjoy a fake winter, where monsoon
exhales through the hollows of window.

Then the sun will leap in its reverie,
flames,
outpours,
bloom,
breeze
and unheard wake-up alarms.

He is a dreamless slumber,
tucked in the bed of satiety.

EFFACING

Which countenance of darkness do you see
when you close your eyes? Can you hear
it the way I do? Eyes buried in the compost
of ears, in the tranquil regurgitations of all
that is capable of loss. These nails have a
tendency to scrape thick dregs of paint behind
our mirrors. But it's still safe to procreate this
illusion: there is no parasite in-between, no
wraith haunting the innards of our silent prayer.
I spend long nights dressed as a tea cosy for
your shoulders; pink-hued, and nearly unseen.
There are moments we dissect our saturnine
hearts, hold them in the crevices of our palms;
the way two scientists discover relics through
a microscope of doubt and announce them ungodly.

DYSPHORIC HEART

Hailstones
are cursed opals clunking
on our frozen landscapes.
There are kittens
in your backyard, swaddling
their mother's congealed blood
around themselves;
returning her spasms
of sacrificial love.
Their death is a cake
lazily rising
in the oven heat.
The last rain of sweat
scurries down
the hull of my clavicles.

PATRIOT

We were deciduous forests, the zephyr of moon, and war.
I watched you lip-synch the music of your culture;
those godwit-in-the-wind gyrations of your feathered cap.
Our kiss a delirious foreplay of waves, and a marooned shanty.
Only in my body, you desired my body, more than your language.
The ruggedness of Himalayas, you reclaimed it; coining
sounds as valedictions in the soft slurs of your caresses.
It was always: my genish, I like your perfume-fragrance,
a polished city girl; your poise is American. The movement
of my lips – your unanswered prayer. You despised my voice,
the crookedness of Urdu phonemes. I was ashamed so I
bid you a litany of tragic flaws. I could cook, but I couldn't
cook you dumpling or aloo garma, it was against the rebellion
I masked in my warm embrace. It's almost inspiring how
you sharpened your passive growls against the whetstone of
traditional values: you loved me with the ibex-soft prosody of
your Burushaski, and that was it – the rhythm was convincing but
the song wasn't. We blossomed like the crust of a cauliflower,
invited love to break us with its ineffable touch; to breathe us back.
Always picking our boomerangs wisely, I bid you my breasts.

Genish (Burushaski): a term of endearment
Aloo garma: traditional dish of Hunza

HATCHING

I am buried inside a cocoon: buried but alive.
My hijab is an opaque sheath I wear like armour:
the brave knight of resilience, call me *a thing* –
a thing of wood designed for the habitual wood
pecker; lover who wins accolades for wielding
his double-edged sword against my woodwork.
I am a histrionic tall-standing trunk, they call me
the Dame of Fortitude; I win accolades for sealing
my lips with the wax of inarticulate letters hung on
my limping boughs; these unrevealed blasphemies,
beautifully veiled. His anarchic sweet-nothings are cold
sherbets gushing out until the unexpected screech of
a faucet, the way a glass shatters between our cemented
walls, and like stormy rains, the crystalline shards
fall on the love-making bed. Over and again.
Hands that love conditionally, touch that twitches the
flesh of my foremothers, and my audacious passivity.

THE DAME OF FORTITUDE

Down her thighs
                      a cavity,

the arches and curls of her fingers;
oblivions stroking a sonogram image,

sonorous is wreckage,

breath churns in a stale umbilicus,

a butter knife
blunt with masculine apathy,

prone to brokenness
or breakability,

cleaves the hull of her navel, invokes
the stillborn daughters of Tutankhamun.

Euthanasia peers through her blush clothing;

calm

the landscapes in her portrait
and dwindling, because the artist

shrivelled to dormancy.

DOMESTICATED

All picture frames have crevices
the size of bloodworms.
Every night his gaze imitates my
straying gaze. I sketch Blakean visions
on my stretch marks: a dream-loop
of arachnids going rampant in the arid
deserts hemming my uterus.
It's truly cumbersome to extract
a revelation from a source of destruction.
Feigned condolences. Buzz kill.
Lilt of songs, lilt of memories.
Drip, dribble, drizzle, drip.
His hands compressing my thighs;
resuscitating an after-life, his helplessness
domesticating my cold unruly grief.

"7–YEAR-OLD GIRL RAPED IN RAWALPINDI"
—A NEWS HEADLINE FROM THE YEAR 2020

> *They've crawled*
> *their way out from behind curtains*
> *of childhood, the silver-pink weight*
> *of their bodies pushing against water,*
> *against the sad, feathered tarnish*
> *of remembrance.*
>
> – TISHANI DOSHI

She wasn't a wilted rose
viciously plucked then
discarded,
a fluttering cherub
bathed in the radiance
of noor,
delicate snow crystal
frothing
in the parched
palms of predators.
Why imprison her in this routinely
lamb-and-the-lion imagery?
A child's not
a breathing thing
waiting to be seized
or trampled down.
Breathing's not an act
of inviting a cut-throat
garrotte
every blue moon.

A rosary.
She was
free
like consciousness,
bold
like femininity.
Not a lynched shard
of meaning
in your passive sentence.
A seven-year-old,
You raped her.

THE GEOGRAPHY OF OUR HISTORY

1.

Back in school,
geography
was earthquakes
and volcanoes,
what makes a river
different from an ocean.
I have always known
the overlooked secret
of nebular women
dancing around stones;
opaque as history,
noxious like the wind
around their song.
Are we the outro to each
landscape we touch?

2.

This house is in extremis,
no plateaus rise above,
roots of a Jamun tree
are hungry appendages
preventing the skeletons
of bricks and rods from
falling apart.
How long do we wait to
witness a downfall?

3.

Some monuments
are bloated landfills
causing a rumpus so
that someone gives
them a proper resting.
The water in my body
craves the space between
the starved midrib
of a poplar, there are
fractures in the
bathroom mirror.
Who is responsible for
waking up the terrains?

4.

Back in school,
geography was
not a fossil of futurity.
Carbon dating
of languages could
have been a forewarning
that mother tongue
is the only misplaced
item in the bulbous
dowry of a daughter,
or that daughters
are monuments
and dowries, never
the appendages.

5.

It's morning.
Sleep is a kind of seepage.
A blizzard is not always a cue
to hide in trenches.
I try not to be a victim
in this poem,
because this is what is
asked of us.
I dab rouge on
my bones,
and leave home
to galvanize the
blizzards.

AFTER YEARS OF DORMANCY

First time in 800 years it erupts,
almost gracefully, akin to a bride
menstruating on her wedding lehenga;
leaving her lover aghast, leaving
his unfulfilled urge in the lit candle
jars of suhaag raat. The headline said,
a volcano awakened in Iceland after
800 years. Awakening is not gentle
like constancy, it barges in the room
with its aches and collateral blemishes.
This time the onlookers cared more
about recording the feisty red rumbles,
but they also cared for the precious life
of the mountain, as if the mountain
belonged to them; the way dowry
belongs to a wolfish starry-eyed groom.
Of course, the men called it sublime;
O the beauty spitting blood and crying.
Of course, the women clenched
their uterus between their hindsight.
They guard it well; the volcanoes erupting
within. How many more 800 years will
it take to flare up and call it what it is?

Lehenga: Bridal attire
Suhaag raat (Urdu/Hindi): wedding night/the night of consummation

THE NIGHTINGALE OF KASHMIR

FOR HABBA KHATOON, THE 16TH CENTURY KASHMIRI POET

The drapes coil away from
Habba khatoon's evergreen laments.
Sweet, cumbersome memory.
Henna fading on immortal flesh.
Love-making inside a poem's refrain;
fate-stained lips sharing blood oaths

then separating.

Four-eyed coyote, blue-eyed
coyote, trinket-eyed lone howl.
Habba Khatoon's banshee-wails;
our treasured ancestral heirlooms.
Love beat again, carry her away.
Come to life her poignant lyres;
scatter hyacinths in her Kashmir.
Call her beloved back, he must
be why death looms in Kashmir.

BODY SPEAKS TWO LANGUAGES

In the coffee shop
rainy jazz violates the loners,
wisps of caffeine
veil the window mists,
I am gift-wrapped with a turquoise
pashmina, my carnivorous anatomy
longing to dance,
this silent patter of chatter around,
willing her back to nascence.

I was told by a poet in passing,
you don't need lessons to dance –
you can just dance.
So I lift up my prosthetic roars,
as if lifting up the floor-licking sequins
of my Mughal gharara,
and I reclaim the coffee shop with
the graceful vulgarity of kathak moves.
Soon the other language
that often speaks for me in
my numbing absence –
the one that over-explains
and wears a vignette of haya
 – ebbs away,
like a lost paparazzi.

Haya (Arabic): Modesty

WEDDING MASHUP

The beat of Punjabi drum, a very masculine bhangra
and the groaning aunties measuring gold and diamonds
with their tongues. A perfect proletarian wedding
with bleats of glitter and palpitating gossips, masala
and all that sugary tarnish of cordial mimicry.
I want to be the most uncalled for blackout;
dark then limned, a cigar I am keen to light up
in the rose bed of aunties and uncles praising
someone's girl for being a doctor who can cook.
Long wisps of smoke respiring through my unchaste
lips, and I am so tired of sitting with my legs crossed,
my ghagra flirting with my stiletto heels,
I am so tired of smiling without a grin. The food
isn't served yet. I smell steaks and the subtle singe
of barbeque, the chilman biryani hiding behind
her inability to express. I am tired of uncles calling me
their pretty daughter only to burn their voyeur-eyes
on my nipples concealed under my silk diamantes dupatta.
'Don't slouch', says an aunty. She runs her fingers through
my hair, measuring the length and femininity conditioned
in these fine purple streaks. Purple is not a graceful colour,
maybe a tinge of blonde or brunette to give the men
a western dream: untouched and impossible to possess.
I am beautiful, beautiful in the way I want to spread
my legs across the table, where Pepsi is served in wine flutes,
and men rape their wives with their eyes and the wives
of their friends. These heels are killing me and the clothes
and the barriers and the uncles and fathers and aunties
and no one cares about the delicately arranged love
between the couple. I yawn, like a gypsy vixen ready

to trot home, without spreading her legs, without
lighting a cigar, without telling the uncle that my nipples
are supple skins trapped inside a lavender brassiere;
trust me it's not an invitation concealed in a metaphor.

Ghagra: traditional formal attire
Chillman Biryani: a special kind of biryani
Bhangra: famous Punjabi dance
Masala (Urdu): Spice

SELF-PORTRAIT AS A GENDERLESS WOMAN

The wind is genderless.
The patriarchs of my land call nature a mother.
A mother is a kaleidoscopic mural, uncontrollable
like the frequency of a broken radio.
I sit in my Daewoo Racer and deep-throat
Cookies n' Cream, soft linens spurting in my mouth.
Here, where I am, I am invisible
like unused china clinking in the kitchen cabinet;
a relic of womanhood from my mother.
My hair, doused in grey palette, resists
the youthfulness of my camel-soft skin.
Women threaten their daughters to stay away,
I am an abandoned lesson on propriety.
This horse cart that gallops past me is a horseless
vehicle, causing a mayhem in the graveyards
beneath Rawalpindi. I think of my eyes;
wild with wayfaring tears. The passive menagerie inside,
raging softly. One has to learn to break the regiments,
to pat the farm-eyed creature, unbraid her sepia mane.
The only way to taste an ice cream is to pronounce
it a sweet felony on the tongue, to become a little less
invisible in the rearview mirror. I don't want to swallow
so soon this genderless woman I am becoming:
a rocket-minaret, thrusting through rocky mounds.

ANTHEM OF THE REBELS IN THE NIGHT

Talking to men at midnight,
some may call it sexting
but I won't. In fact, I can't.
And if you ask me, yes
I want to repel my urges,
exile them in the shameless
fires, dance on the embers with
everything raving inside me.
Of course, my breasts.
Don't we need this kind of reprieve?
A misshapen joy tickling
the wild beasts under our feet.
At night when our forefathers sleep
with reins swaddling around
their hands, we break free, turn
up the music; Florence + the Machine,
loud and faithless, like veins
throbbing in our necks, our vulvas.
She-wolves howling at the blood moon.
Pretty faces, prettier bodies.
Our reflections like running waters.
Tongues parched. Cunnilingus.
At night we are born as sadists,
all of us. In the carmine skirts
of vulgarity, we cradle shy desires
in spiky palms, callous gazes.
Drinks dripping, tossing these shadows
of us in the witch-fire, each log of
wood the crimson in our hymen;
clogged and festooned with tradition.
At night we creep out of the potholes
of virtue, carrying the torches,

binoculars, and pliers. Young sleuths,
old sleuths, looking for things to
dismantle. Our grumbling magma
smouldering the culprits who stole
our voice-guns. We too can jolt you
out of these uninvited axioms
drooling from your Caligula-mouths:
betiyan achi houn tou izzat, aur buri
houn tou maa baap per bojh hain.*
At night, we are girls and women,
we are brazen verbs of every action,
the bangle-jingling iconoclasts;
we are the fairy lights of resurgence.

*Good daughters bring honour, bad daughters are a burden on their parents.

IV

VI

VERBIS DIABLO

Mammon
now lurks in English dactyls,
stressed syllables
untethering the bonds
of stout Punjabi ragas.
The accentuated *errs* and *oh my gods*,
and the most misconstrued *like*
like the invisible cries of Habba Khatoon,
lost in translation,
lost in the history of voice
when voice was not a political strum.
She is a poet because she wiped her tears
with the cadence of language.
At Maghrib the muezzin gargles
with Arabic verses.
The English teacher at school;
slick as a barouche-landau,
drunk with the scent of Marilyn Monroe,
siphons Urdu from our dreams.
True splendour is in performing wuzu
with impurities usurping the throats.

Wuzu: (Islamic) ablution

BLUE MOON

In winter, I think of a refugee;
an Afghan girl like desert wind,
with golden eyes of a coyote

She is collecting firewood
somewhere, 'somewhere'
has become an anagram for her

The passers-by watch her
giggle through the untrammelled
threads in her ghost-white dupatta

She has killed another beetle,
it is now a searing inscription
underneath her plastic slippers

KILL THE REFUGEE

When you see a newborn refugee,
first, let your eyes peer through metal
barricades, the sky a glaring tangerine
blending in the seams of malnourished
cityscapes. You may have never seen with
your bare eyes the ululations of a family
forced to abandon its grave; the soil
of the homeland is a native's great beyond.
Imagine not being able to die at the time
of your death, someone has to dodge
Azrael's all four faces to stay on Earth,
become a landfill of memorabilia,
a creature of yore. Look, a different kind
of man lived here, reduced to a different
kind of rubble. Look, the ruins don't
speak the language of home. Of homeliness.
It happens sooner than later, underneath
the scintillating Canopus, your grandma's
cutlery submits to the staccato of
someone else's kitchen-table jargon.
The objects are diagnosed with amnesia.
That bisque ceramic teapot and the abluted
prayer rug, and the dog-eared calendar,
and your father's unused musket sagging by
the wall; now face a brand new qiblah.
Perhaps, even god had to remember what
he is made of, what he left behind
before pronouncing himself omniscient.
It only takes a billion years to chant
the names of your belongings before
losing them to this news, say, on a radio
in a burgundy Alto; which then seems

like the only place where homesickness
is not a deliberate crime. Remembrance
is exorcism. You don't know which
demon of geography you will summon
when you saunter inside a bereft thought.
You have to ask yourself,
are we allowed to mourn?
The next time you go to a playground
and you see a newborn refugee;
weary shadow of an Afghan boy kicking
plastic bottles on the dirt of Rawalpindi,
his shalwar flapping; one brisk kick at a time
in the dark of daylight: you should muster up
the courage to kill the refugee, the Afghan,
the boy, the threat. Then call him a child,
your very own. Return him the tears, his tears.

ORIGINS OF HUMANKIND
FOR PALESTINE

There are things bigger than pandemic:
a bullet between your ribs, faint whir
of bomb before explosion. Suddenly the core
of our planet belches histories
of nemeses; blue-ringed, their eyes
lightsabers rimmed by aconite, slashing through
meditative herons, through slow-breathing debris.
Who could have thought that the virus
had no power to plague an array of corpses?
Severed heads over shoes, over black cats that
are silenced by bigger omens; slowly suffusing the
air, the bone marrow. Soon the minarets sing
of writhing helicopters. Reveries are
in stasis. A child is rescuing his cat from
a dying lustre. There are people holding onto
meaning smaller than the size of a virus;
weighing salt in pepper shakers.
Language too can stumble in as a blind seer
and tell you there are no time aberrations
where children skydive over trampolines,
catching star-tailed missiles,
washing off bombardments,
succumbing.

THE AFTER-WORLD

My little cousin sits in front of the TV,
his knees still, toes clenched
like marine-frozen echinoderms,
his clueless mind wandering
the Teletubbyland, a salivary giggle,
holophrastic utterances sledding in the room.
His mother channels her motherly voice
to stop him from sucking his thumb;
a motherly growl.
Then the indifference susurrates.
His dad wipes his glasses,
he is always wiping objects
as if they are a kind of aberration.
Houses are built so that the inhabitants
can learn to deceive time.
Someone is watching them
from the satellites of man-god,
they are someone's laboratory samples.
Connotation is a headphone blocking
the outside world
when the outside world is cleaved
from the inside, when the world outside
is stripped of its interiority,
when committing a crime is truly just,
just a catchy proverb for someone
who spilled tea before pouring it in a cup.

FRIDAY NIGHT ON MURREE ROAD

Tonight we are playing
gun-to-your-head in a traffic jam.
Blueberry has stopped blinking his
raven eyes when we echo his name;
he knows he will die long before
the vet pronounces him dead,
is this not the holiest way
to depart the temporal realm?
A politician is leading a protest,
snickering at his rival's bald head;
his followers indoctrinated
to gleam with rivers of tears.
The road is a giant slogan
of misery in capital letters.
Fruit sellers are in a minor scuffle
with their customers, oranges
and tangerines and clementines;
one has to taste them to decide
the primal taste of corruption.
A thirsty hound drinks water
from the gutter like it's blood.
The siren of an ambulance breaks
like dawn, breaks like fresh breath.

STRANGE OBJECTS IN THE SKY

Attention, there was a UFO sighting by
the PIA pilots in the Karachi skies,

or so we believe.

The soothsayers who play with numbers

and sacred verses,

heard the news with blessing gallivanting
in their eyes; as if the UFO wasn't an agenda
concealed in the profanities of the wind,

they smiled

with all their religion and faith, preached
that it was the holy archangel's noor;
the luminescence that saved our passengers
from an imminent catastrophe.

But the scientists

who have studied numbers, who often quantify
their intuitions, called the UFO an artificial planet
or a space station or anything where reason could
save them from the red herrings clogging their larynx.

Dream-makers found a story:

if it's an angel, it will be the devil in disguise,
if it's a spaceship; the aliens will look like humans
or they won't look from their eyes.

The dream-makers called it nothing,

believed in the mist,

spurred longing, relighted the miracle of curiosity
in a ten-year-old to stargaze on his rooftop

until the unthinkable

comes to incipience, until a pilot dares to fly
straight into the UFO, uniting with a solar flare.
One moment the child points at the sky

and traces the anomaly,

then he grows weary of it, and soon he drifts
into his sublunary requiems.

RENASCENCE OF DESTRUCTION

Math is irrelevant to nature,
what exists, exists without
the need for stratification, without
oscillating curves or whole numbers
bridging gaps between humans and
unidentified microcosms

Rebirth will live as a sun-basking
myth in ouroboros if it counts the
instances it swallows its tail

It all comes down to one fish in
stasis, wafting over bubonic shore
letting oceanic life ebb and flow around it,
the giddy platonic lover

The same shore is home to fishermen
glaring at sunny bonfires, fishing for furtive
ancestral tales, these betel-spitting
loud thinkers of "nothing comes from nothing"
these god-fearing believers of rebirth
being a soft-whispered euphemism for
renascence of destruction

If a plastic bag sways and flutters several times
against the wind: it is still no vicar of happiness,
the life inside it is only a life trapped inside;
breathless, and out of breath.

REMEMBERING A REPRESSED MEMORY

A squirrel smacks its tail
deep into the blue lagoon;
signalling the darkness.
An ice sculpture rises
like the great Loch Ness
from a pale blue bassinet
nearby, broken to its bone.
Soon somebody spills
all the names of a Jane Doe.
A gazelle grunts in the quiet
corner of endless bickering.
Remember when Gatsby
cradled that vintage crystal in
the tragedies of his eyes?
It's that kind of night on the
hills of copulating memories.
A single gunshot wound.
Somewhere is a propensity,
craning its neck to read
the day's paper, gasping at
murder mysteries, gently
sauntering back and forth;
a god lost in a city of skyscrapers.

MINDFUL BREATHING

Not every misfortune is a bland warning.
Night is swinging like the shadow
of a hammock, quit calling it an allegory
on Oedipus' blindness. Some bruises
are silhouettes of lost wayfarers,
like the ones of our parents;
harrowing but only from a distance.
To wander with an air of bliss
is to imitate the perennial magnolias
in every other ghost-garden home.

Take off your tinted glasses, witness
the miracle of three moons effervescing
in the flamingo sky, breathe out.

ACKNOWLEDGEMENTS

Grateful acknowledgement is made to the editors of the magazines, journals, anthologies and micro-chapbook for publishing the following poems:

Visual Verse: "Nascence", "Temporal Glitch", "Crescendo", "Effacing", "Renascence of Destruction" (Volume 07: Chapter 08, 10 and 11; Volume 08: Chapter 08 and 10)

The Punch Magazine: "The Caged Bird Rehearses before it Sings", "Portrait of a Photographer as a Historian", "Outro to Grief", "Kill the Refugee", "Ode to a Nurse", "Wedding Mashup"

The Wild Word: "A Postcard from My Mother Who Met Death in the Most Startling Way" "Prelude"

The Ofi Press: "Coronacation"

New Feathers Anthology: "Morning Prayer" (First Runner-up for the New Feathers Award 2021)

Origami Poems Project (Grief is a Firefly, 2021): "Empty Threat", "Penumbra", "House of Dissociation"

Ink, Sweat and Tears: "Cloudage"

Raconteur Review: "Clamped"

Fragmented Voices: "Dysphoric Heart"

Autumn Sky Poetry DAILY: "Desiderium"

Women's Spiritual Poetry Project: "The Vicissitudes of Self"

Feminist Voices Anthology Volume 2: "Hatching"

The Aleph Review: "7-year-old Girl Raped in Rawalpindi: a news headline from the year 2020"

Eunoia Review: "Bread Crumbs", "Self-Portrait as a Genderless Woman", "Ghost Town", "Dissecting the End of My Day"

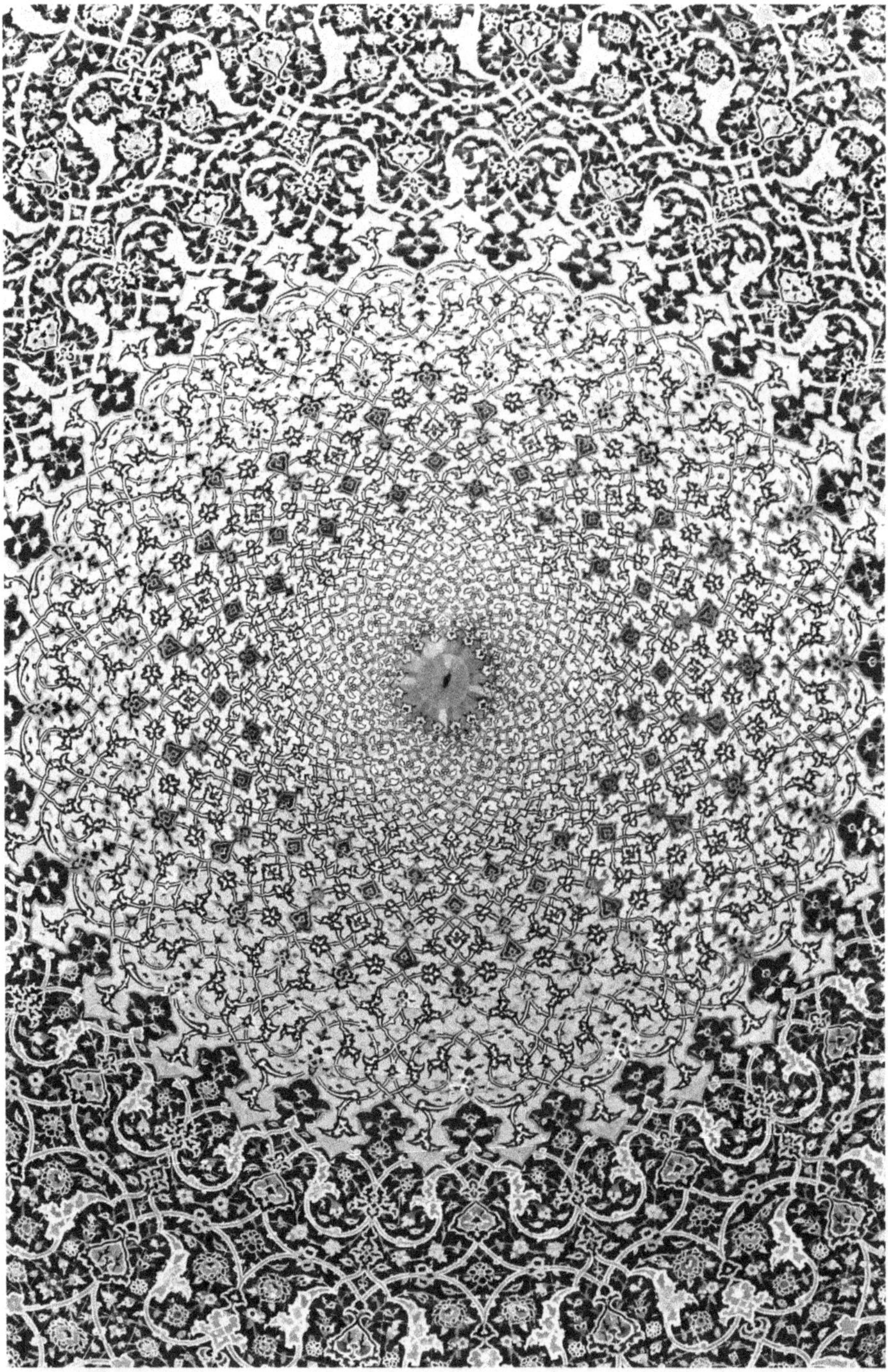

www.ingramcontent.com/pod-product-compliance
Lightning Source LLC
LaVergne TN
LVHW041634070426
835507LV00008B/614